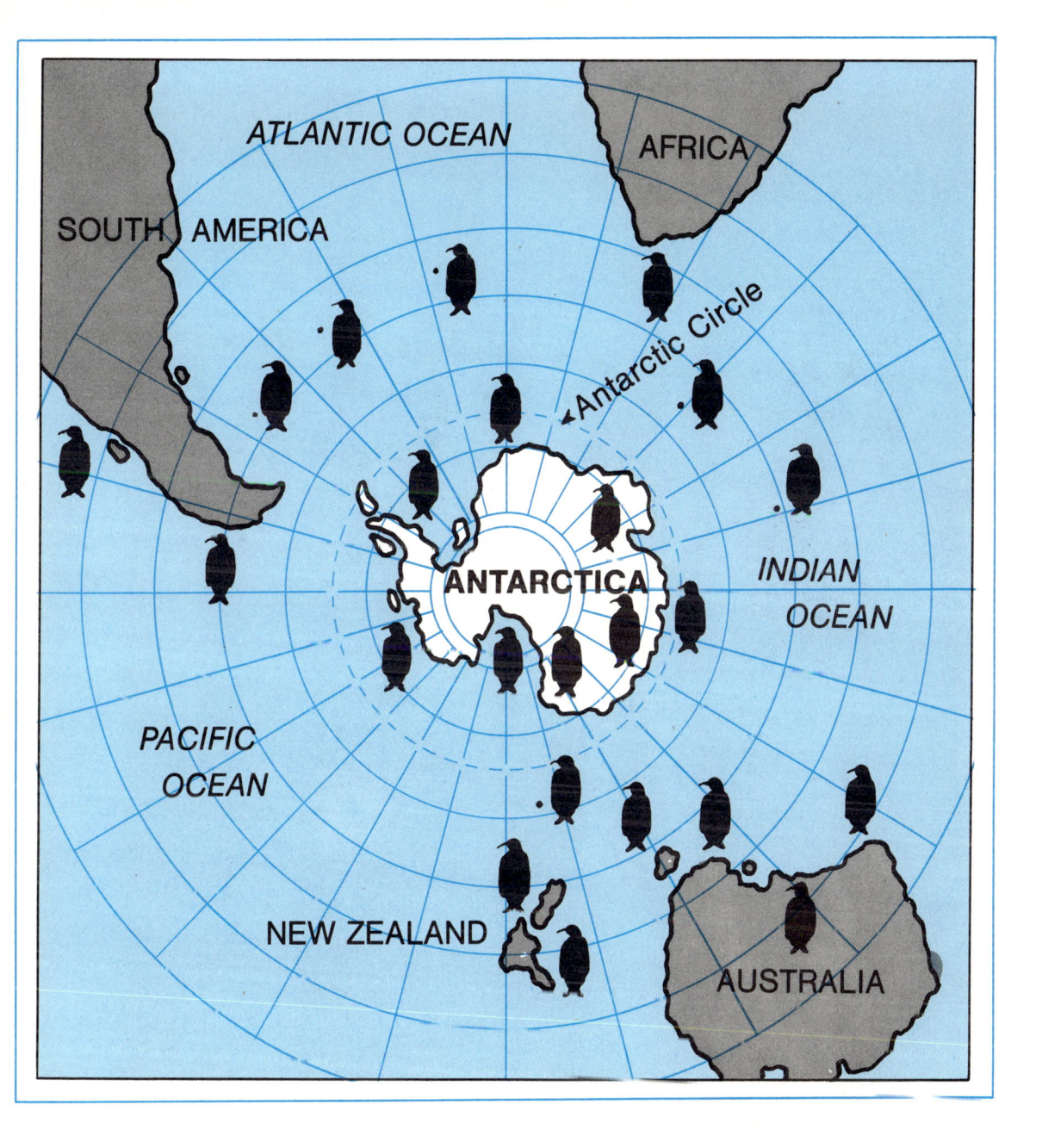

There are seventeen different kinds of penguins. All of them live in the southern half of the world as shown on this map. The emperor penguins live in Antarctica, near the South Pole.

Pen
Emperor Penguin

By Sally Glendinning

Drawings by Arabelle Wheatley

GARRARD PUBLISHING COMPANY
CHAMPAIGN, ILLINOIS

Photo Credits

Michael Castellini, Physiological Research Laboratory,
  Scripps Institution of Oceanography: pp. 6, 15
Robert W. Hernandez/National Audubon Society Collection/
  Photo Researchers: p. 31
G. L. Kooyman, Physiological Research Laboratory, Scripps
  Institution of Oceanography: pp. 34, 35
Roger Tory Peterson/National Audubon Society Collection/
  Photo Researchers: p. 22
Michael Rougier, Life Magazine, © Time, Inc.: pp. 2, 28
Michael C. T. Smith/National Audubon Society Collection/
  Photo Researchers: pp. 11, 21
U. S. Navy photo: pp. 9, 12, 19, 25

Map on page 1 by Benjamin C. Blake

Library of Congress Cataloging in Publication Data

Glendinning, Sally.
   Pen, emperor penguin.

  (Young Animal Adventures)
  SUMMARY: Describes the life of an Emperor penguin from his birth through his first year of life.
   1. Emperor penguin—Juvenile literature.
[1. Emperor penguin. 2. Penguins] I. Wheatley, Arabelle. II. Title.
QL696.S473G53   598.4'41   80-13212
ISBN 0-8116-7500-9

Copyright © 1980 by Sally Glendinning.   All rights reserved.   Manufactured in the U.S.A.

Pen: Emperor Penguin

The biggest penguin climbed to the top of a snow-covered hill. He stood alone, looking up at the gray sky. It was getting dark, for soon winter would come.

The big penguin was four feet tall. He weighed almost 90 pounds. He looked like a man dressed for a party in a black silk coat and pants. His black feathers shone. His fat belly was soft and white, like a man's shirt.

The emperor is the biggest and most colorful of all penguins. Male and female look alike.

On each side of his head were bright yellow patches. The downy feathers under his chin were pale yellow. There was a rose-colored stripe along the lower part of his bill. This handsome bird was an emperor penguin.

He cawed and clucked and whistled as penguins do. He knew that winter was coming, and it was time to go home.

He looked down the hill. A few other penguins were standing there. He flopped down on his white belly and slid down the hill like a sled. He used his stiff wings to push himself even faster.

Then he stood up on his big feet. He waddled over to the other penguins. It was time for them to go home.

Emperor penguins live on the ice-covered land called Antarctica, around the South Pole.

When penguins are tired or in a hurry, they flop down on their bellies and "row" with their feet.

Each summer they swim, fish, and play in the sea near the coast. They also walk for many miles over the ice-covered land. In the fall, when the bright light fades from the sky, they return to their homes. Their homes are called rookeries, and hundreds of emperor penguins live in each rookery. Year after year, each group of penguins returns to the same rookery just before winter comes.

The biggest penguin stood straight and tall as the others cawed and clucked at one another. Then he started off. One by one, the others followed. They marched along in a single line, taking short steps. They never seemed to grow tired as they slowly followed their leader toward their rookery.

More penguins joined the line along the way. Soon there were hundreds of the big

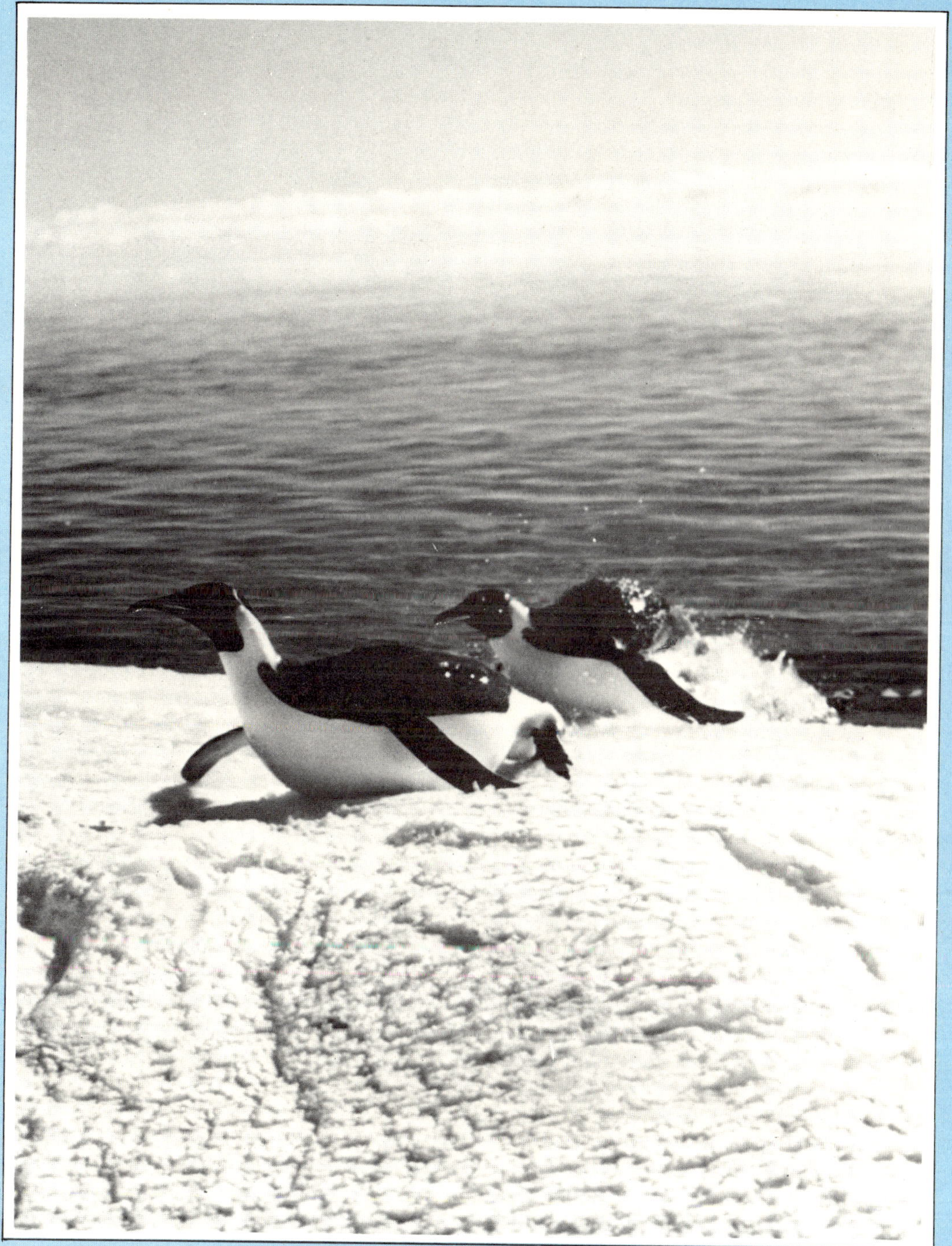

The hills of ice behind this rookery help to keep out the freezing winds.

birds in the long line. Home was far away, but the emperor penguins never got lost. They never took time to look for food. They had learned long ago to get all their food from the sea, for there was nothing to eat on the ice.

At last the penguins were nearly home. The ice in their rookery was thousands of feet deep. Hills of ice nearby helped protect the penguins from howling winter winds.

Many other penguins were already there when the big penguin led his group into the rookery. The penguins made little sounds and bowed to one another. It was a happy time, for the emperor penguins were glad to be home.

The biggest penguin looked for his mate. He knew she would be waiting for him. He went from one penguin to another. He sang his own special song and waited for his mate to

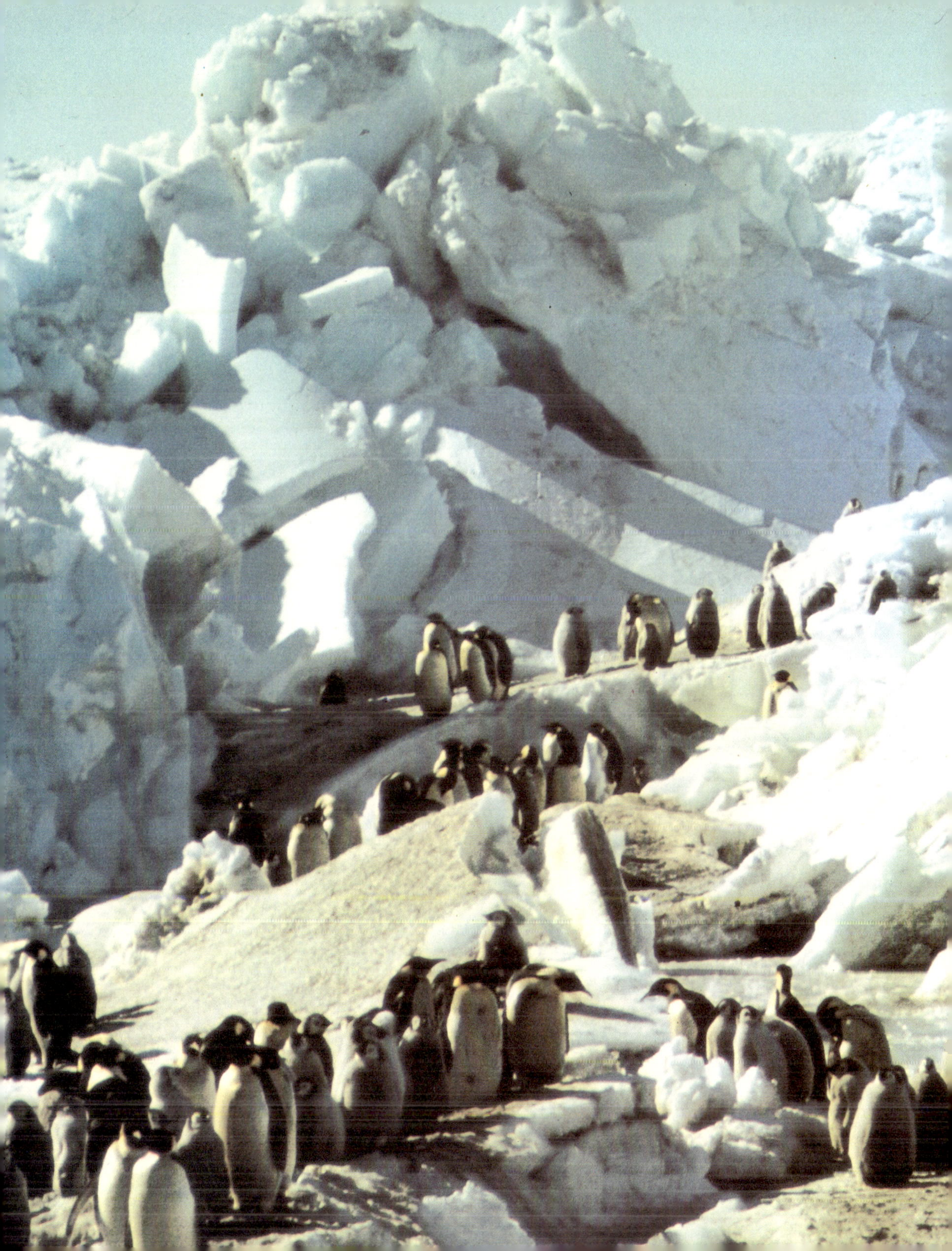

answer. Was it this one? No. Was it that one?

Finally he found her. Another penguin was singing to her. The biggest penguin went over to them. He clucked and whistled. He fussed angrily at the other penguin. He tossed his head. At last the stranger left.

Although emperor penguins are very good fighters, they do not fight each other.

The biggest penguin sang and bowed to his mate. She made soft little sounds in reply. He reached out his long beak to touch her feathers. He danced about on his big feet. He was telling her that he was happy to see her again.

Soon it was dark, for winter had come. The sun would not shine for many weeks. This was the time when they mated and each female penguin would lay an egg. Soon there would be a family—a mother, a father, and a baby penguin chick. This was the happiest time of the year for the emperor penguins.

The emperor penguins did not build nests. There were no twigs, no leaves, no bits of grass on the ice-covered rookery floor. When the time came, the mother penguin laid her egg on the ice. Then she cuddled the egg between her feet and her soft belly to keep it warm.

The father penguin stood beside the mother. In a little while, the mother pushed the egg toward him. He held it on his feet, protecting it with the warm feather pad under his belly. He knew he had to keep the egg warm so the baby penguin inside could grow.

Each father penguin held an egg on his feet. When the mother penguins saw that the eggs were safe, they left. They went to find food in the sea far away. There was nothing for them to eat on the ice at home.

The father penguins would have no food for two long months. The fat stored inside their bodies would keep them alive.

It was cold and dark. The wind howled around the icy hills. It became even colder.

Females are going to the sea to find fish.
The males stay behind to care for the eggs.

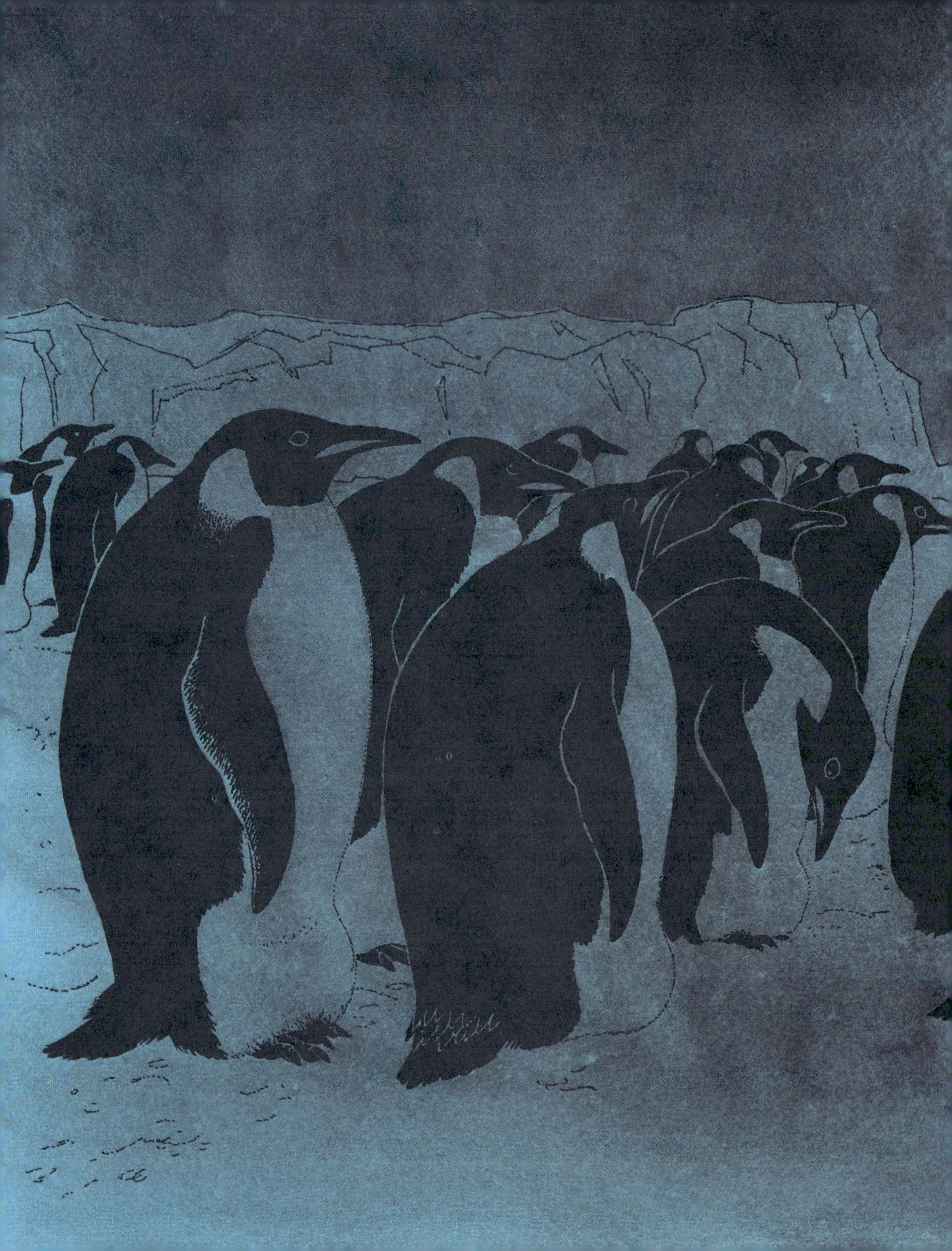

The father penguins moved slowly toward each other to keep warm. They huddled together in little groups with their backs to the wind.

One father moved his foot too far. The egg rolled off his foot and froze on the ice. The father made sad cries. He tried to get the egg back onto his feet, but it was too late. He knew the baby penguin inside the egg was dead.

The biggest penguin held his egg carefully. He was hungry and cold, but he didn't mind. As long as the egg was safe, nothing else mattered. Soon there would be a penguin chick.

At last the mother penguins came home from the sea. They knew it was time for the eggs to hatch. The mother penguins were fat, for they had eaten many fish. They had eaten enough tiny, tiny fish called krill to feed the penguin chicks.

Mother Penguin waddled as fast as she could to where Father Penguin stood. He still had the egg tucked safely on his feet, under his pad of feathers. Pen, their baby penguin, was inside the egg. For many hours he had been trying to get out.

Pen pecked on the shell with his sharp little beak. The eggshell cracked a little.

"Kaa-a-a, kaa-a-a," Pen cried. Finally, Pen broke through the shell. He pushed his little head outside the warm feather pad for a moment. He looked like a round gray ball covered with soft down. He was cold, for his downy baby feathers were not enough to keep him warm.

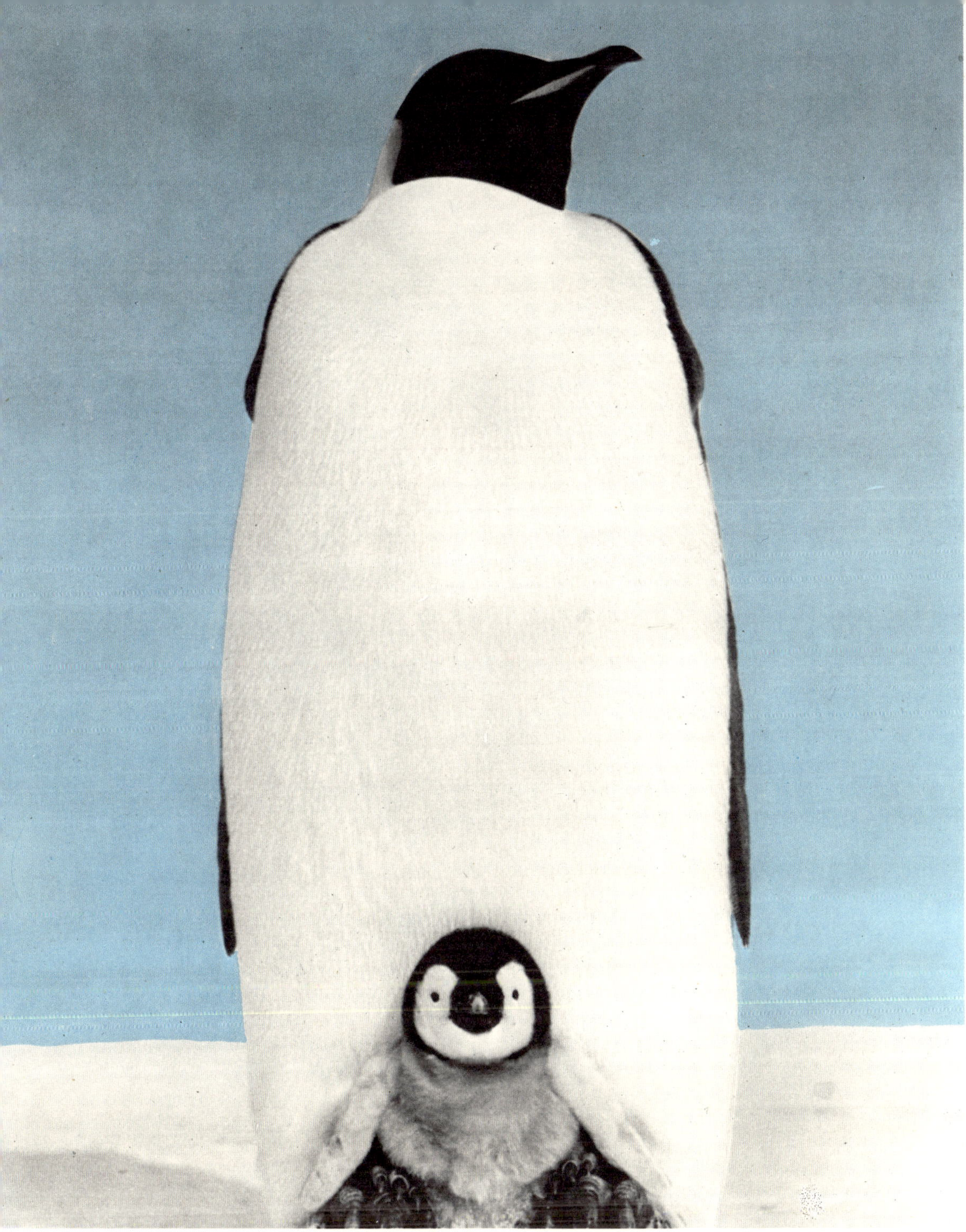

This chick is a few months old.
He can walk on the ice by himself.

The biggest penguin bent low to touch Pen with his beak. He made soft cawing sounds and gave a whistle. He was proud and happy.

Then Mother took Pen on her feet. She held him close under her belly to keep him warm. She bent her head low, opened her beak, and forced up some of the krill she had eaten. Pen stuck his head inside her beak to get the food.

"Kaa-a-a!" Pen cried happily. He liked the krill. He reached inside his mother's beak for some more.

Now the biggest penguin and the other fathers left the rookery. It was their turn to feed on fish from the sea. When they had eaten all they wanted, they would return home.

Pen was bigger than the other penguin chicks. As he grew, Mother and Father took turns going to the sea for food. They always brought home plenty of fish for Pen to eat.

During the spring months, soft gray light came back to the sky. Then the gray color turned to pale blue. One day the first rays of the sun appeared. Later the sun rose in the sky once more. The air was cold, but the penguins knew that spring had come because the sun was shining.

Pen no longer had to stand on the feet of his

The red on the chick's wing and neck
was painted there by a scientist who was studying
emperor penguins in the Antarctic.

father or mother. He began to walk around on the ice by himself. Sometimes his feet slipped, and he sat down hard.

One day it was time for Mother and Father to go together to the sea. There they would swim, eat, and frolic in the cold water. Pen was still too small to go with them.

As Mother and Father started off, Pen ran after them on his short legs. "Kaa-a-a!" he cried. But it was no use. He had to stay at home with the other penguin chicks. Some of the big penguins stayed at home, too. They would care for the penguin chicks until the parents returned.

The big penguins tried to keep the chicks near them. When the little ones wandered away, the big penguins clucked and scolded them. The big penguins were warning the little ones that a skua might fly down and grab one of them. The little penguins understood that a skua might harm them, so they stayed near the big penguins.

One day Pen saw a giant bird in the sky high above his head. He was frightened, for he had never seen such a big bird. He wondered if it was a skua. He ran close to one of the big penguins. They were not worried about the big bird in the sky.

The big bird was a mollymawk. It spread its giant wings and sailed through the air like a kite. It was riding on the wind currents. As the wind pushed it along, the mollymawk tilted to one side and then to the other. It moved across the sky like a gray cloud.

Pen wanted to fly like a mollymawk. He held out his stiff little wings and waited for

The big penguins are baby-sitting for the chicks while the chicks' parents are away.

the wind to sweep him into the air. Nothing happened.

Pen soon learned from the big penguins that emperor penguins can't fly. But Pen kept on trying. He ran on his little legs and tried to jump into the air. Instead, he fell flat on his belly. He tried and tried again.

Pen was so busy trying to fly that he forgot about the skuas. He also forgot to stay close to the big penguins.

One day he was playing near the penguin egg that had rolled from the father's feet many weeks ago. The egg still lay frozen on the ice. Pen didn't see the brown bird that landed near him and began to peck on the egg. The fierce-looking bird had golden feathers under its neck. It looked at Pen with its beady eyes and reached for him with its sharp claws.

Suddenly Pen saw the brown bird. He was too frightened to run. It was a skua! The skua's claws touched Pen's feathers. Pen leaned back, fell on the ice, and rolled away.

A big penguin had been looking for Pen. He saw that Pen was in trouble and ran between him and the skua. The penguin squawked and whistled. He hit the skua with his wing. The skua flew away.

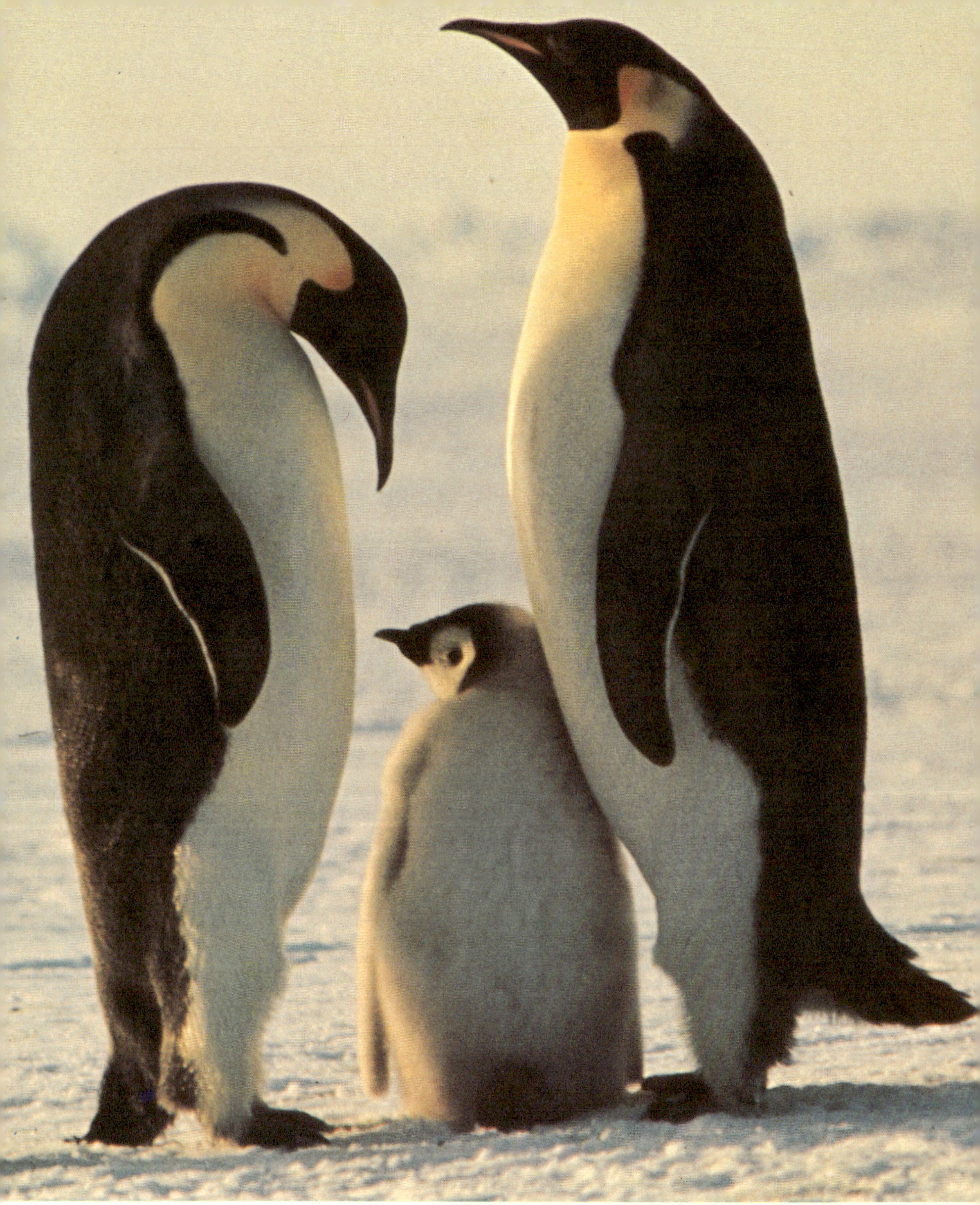

A penguin chick snuggles close to one parent while the other parent watches.

Just then, Mother and Father Penguin returned from the sea. Mother Penguin had food for Pen, but he was too frightened to eat. He pushed his little round head close to his mother. Finally she fed him. He stood near her for a long time.

Each day the sunlight grew brighter as Pen grew bigger. His feathers began to grow through the down that had covered him as a baby. Before long he began to look like his father. Pen was not a baby chick any longer.

One day, Father Penguin let Pen know that he could go on a trip to the sea. Pen was very happy. He danced about on the ice.

Soon all the young penguins started off with their parents. It was a long way for the young penguins to walk. Finally, they reached the water. Pen stood with the others on the edge of the ice and looked at the deep blue sea. Big pieces of ice floated on the water.

Just then a big sea animal came out of the water and jumped onto the ice. It lay down near Pen. It rolled its big eyes to look at him. The sea animal was gray with dark spots.

Pen was frightened. He let out a squawk, and Father Penguin ran to him. Father cawed and clucked and whistled. Pen learned that the big animal was a leopard seal. He learned that leopard seals seldom harm emperor penguins on the ice. Even so, Pen was careful not to stand too close to the seal. The big leopard seal closed its eyes and went to sleep.

Pen stood there looking at the seal. He learned that leopard seals are dangerous in the water. They chase penguins and eat little penguins and big ones, too.

Penguins fear leopard seals more when they hide in the water hoping to catch a careless penguin.

The seal slept for a long time. Then Pen watched while the seal slid into the water and swam away.

Before long it was time for the penguins to feed. Together, they splashed down into the cold water. Pen went in with the rest. He was surprised that he could swim! Swimming was more fun than trying to fly. He used his stiff wings like flippers to spin himself around in the water. He gulped down a few little fish. He even swam under some big pieces of ice. He came up with a splash and jumped back onto the shore.

One day Pen saw a huge animal in the water. It was many times bigger than the leopard seal. The animal's back was shining black, and its belly was white. It had a big white patch over each eye. Pen learned that the animal was a killer whale. He knew that he must stay far away from killer whales, for they liked to eat seals and penguins.

The penguins liked to swim together. The old ones and the young penguins went into the water at the same time. They ate plenty of fish and played for a while. Then they all left the water together. Pen and the other young penguins liked to dive deep, spin about, and

Penguins love to swim and play in the water. They can swim under the water for as long as eighteen minutes before coming up for air.

On page 35, the penguin is jumping out of the water onto the ice.

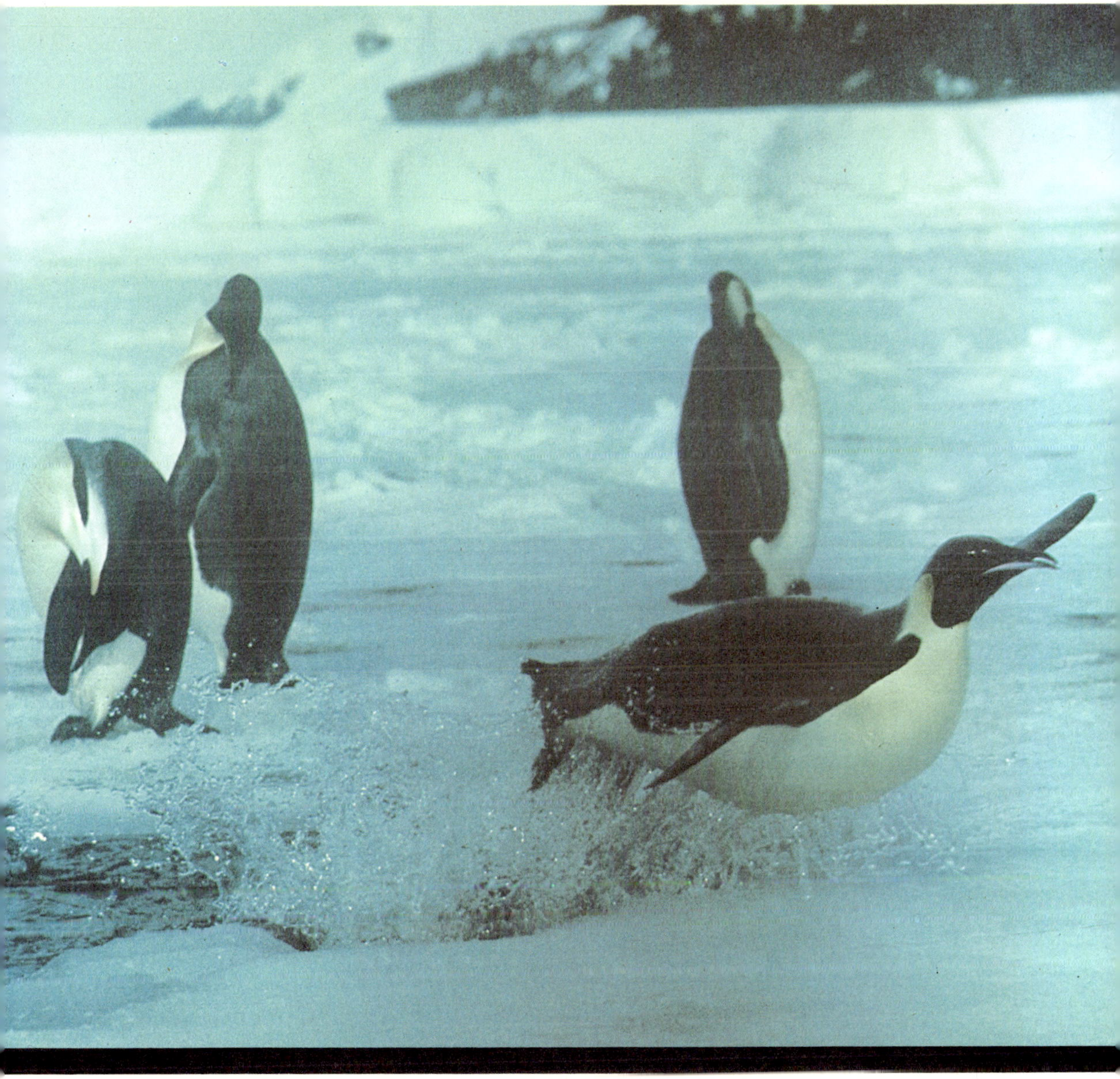

shoot back up through the cold water. They never swam alone, for they knew there was safety in numbers.

Pen's mother loved the water, too. She always wanted to go back in for one last swim. One day she stood on the shore and looked down into the water. She knew she shouldn't swim alone. Pen watched as she jumped into the water.

A leopard seal was hiding under the ice near the shore. Pen saw the seal swim toward his mother. The seal's jaws were wide open as he reached out for her. Mother Penguin knew the seal could swim faster than she could. So she spread her flippers and made a quick turn. The seal did not catch her. Then Mother Penguin tucked her flippers against her sides and pushed hard. She jumped out of the water and landed on the shore. The leopard seal tried to jump after her. But he was too large to jump as far as Mother Penguin. The leopard seal slipped back into the water.

Mother Penguin gasped and sputtered. Father Penguin and Pen scolded her for swimming alone.

Now the sun shone all the time. Some of the emperor penguins left the group and went their different ways. A few of them walked along the shore, looking for a new place to swim and hunt for fish. Others went off on little trips across the ice-covered land.

One day a big piece of ice broke away from the shore. Mother Penguin hopped on it for a ride. She would see Father Penguin and Pen at home next winter.

Father and Pen went off together for a long

walk. In the distance, they saw two men. The men had come to Antarctica to study the birds. They wore wool caps, thick jackets, and warm boots. They wore dark brown glasses to protect their eyes from the light.

Father and Pen walked close to the men. Pen walked over to one of them and looked into his face.

The man reached out to stroke Pen's feathers. Pen didn't like that. He hit the man with his wing.

Father and Pen wandered away. They walked for a long time, until they reached a snow-covered hill. They climbed to the top of the hill and stood there for a few minutes. Then Father Penguin flopped down on his belly and slid down the hill. Pen flopped down and pushed off with his flippers. He and his father zoomed down the hill like two sleds. What fun it was! Pen wanted to climb the hill again and again so he could slide down.

Pen and his father would have a fine trip together. But they would know when it was time to go home to the rookery, where Mother Penguin would be waiting for them. By that time, Pen would be big enough to take care of himself through the next long, cold winter.

Index

Antarctica, 1 (map), 7, 38

Emperor penguins
 baby-sitters, 23, 25 (pic)
 chicks, 13, 17, 20-21, 22 (pic), 23-24, 25 (pic), 28 (pic)
 courtship, 10, 12, 13
 description, 5, 7
 eggs, 13-14, 15, 17-18, 26
 enemies, 24, 26-27, 30, 31 (pic), 32-33, 36-37
 food and feeding, 10, 14, 15 (pic), 17-18, 20, 21, 29, 32-33
 home, 7, 8, 10, 20
 migration, 7, 8

Fish, 8, 18, 20, 21, 33, 37

Killer whale, 33

Leopard seal, 30, 31 (pic), 32, 33, 36-37

Mollymawk, 24

Rookery, 8, 10, 11, 13, 20, 39

Skua, 24, 26-27

South Pole, 7